Rap Your W

T0276652

RAPPING Rhymes about Friends

Thomas Kingsley Troupe

BLACK
RABBIT
BOOKS

Hi Jinx is published by Black Rabbit Books
P.O. Box 3263, Mankato, Minnesota, 56002.
www.blackrabbitbooks.com
Copyright © 2021 Black Rabbit Books

Jen Besel, editor; Michael Sellner, designer;
Omay Ayres, photo researcher

Library of Congress Cataloging-in-Publication Data
Names: Troupe, Thomas Kingsley, author.
Title: Rapping rhymes about friends /
Thomas Kingsley Troupe.
Description: Mankato, Minnesota : Black Rabbit
Books, [2021] | Series: Hi jinx. Rap your world |
Includes bibliographical references. |
Audience: Ages 8-12. | Audience: Grades 4-6. |
Summary: Explores the world of friendship
through poems meant for rapping. Includes
suggestions for how to create raps about friends.
Identifiers: LCCN 2019026711 (print) |
LCCN 2019026712 (ebook) |
ISBN 9781623103217 (hardcover) |
ISBN 9781644664179 (paperback) |
ISBN 9781623104153 (adobe pdf) |
Subjects: LCSH: Friendship—Juvenile poetry. | Children's
poetry, American. | CYAC: Friendship—Poetry. |
American poetry.
Classification: LCC PS3620.R6825 R37 2021 (print) |
LCC PS3620.R6825 (ebook) | DDC 811/.6—dc23
LC record available at https://lccn.loc.gov/2019026711
LC ebook record available at https://lccn.loc.gov/2019026712

Printed in the United States. 1/20

Image Credits

Alamy: BNP Design Studio, 12–13; Dreamstime: Isaac Marzioli, 12;
iStock: Adelevin, 4; Big_Ryan, 2–3; kennykiernan, 15; Shutterstock:
ADudkov, 3, 21; akarakingdoms, 12; Alena Kozlova, 16; Aluna1,
14; anfisa focusova, 13; Angeliki Vel, 19; Arcady, 1; balabolka, 11;
Christopher Hall, Cover, 3, 4, 7, 8, 11, 12, 15, 16, 19, 20; Cory
Thoman, 11; Denis Cristo, Cover, 4-5, 6–7, 23; DRogatnev, 12–13;
Dualororua, 11; KennyK.com, 20; Liron Peer, 12; Lorelyn Medina,
18, 19; mejnak, 10; Memo Angeles, 9, 10, 11, 16, 17, 21; mickallnice,
15; opicobello, 11; Pasko Maksim, 15, 23, 24; penang, 1; pitju, 5, 19,
21; Ron Dale, 5, 8, 12, 16, 20; Ron Leishman, 14–15, 16–17; Sergey
Bogdanov, Cover; Simakova Elena, 10; STREET STYLE, Cover, 1, 4;
totallypic, 17; Tueris, Cover, 1, 15; Vector memory, 20; Verzzh, 8;
your, 16; Every effort has been made to contact copyright holders for
material reproduced in this book. Any omissions will be rectified in
subsequent printings if notice is given to the publisher.

Contents

Chapter 1

Rap Your World!

Yo, listen up readers! Who are the peeps you defend,

The ones you talk to or play with or spend the weekend?

Those people are friends, and they make the world fun.

Let's rap about the relationships that

can't be outdone.

Have you ever had a buddy, a mate, or a pal?

There are lots of names for friends, be it a guy or a gal.

People you hang with when you're looking for fun,

Rapping about friends? Yo, you know we've just begun!

We'll rap about the friends who live down your block,

And the ones who get real sweaty and smell like a sock.

Let's rhyme about the friends you've known all these years,

What's the purpose of this book? To celebrate **peers**!

Chapter 2
Making Friends

Some people meet friends right in their neighborhood,

Saying hey, how you doing, how's it going, what's good?

It's always nice to have a friend who lives right next door,

Think of all the fun you'll have—adventures **galore**!

Friends don't magically appear; please don't think I'm a fool,

Many will be in that learning spot—I'm talking about school.

When you're on a break from science and **arithmetic**,

Have lunch with some friends whose **personalities** click!

You can make friends with people out playing sports,

In the pool, on the field, or on the basketball courts.

Doing your best to compete and to show off your skill,

Giving high-fives to your pals Aidan, Tess, and Jamil.

The most popular sport in the world is soccer.

Some of our friends live on the other side of the earth,

And can tell you what a **peso** or a **yen** is worth.

Keep in touch with these pals by letter or computer,

A smiley face on the envelope? Yo, it couldn't be cuter.

Chapter 3
Hanging with Friends

Having fun with our pals is as easy as it seems.

One thing we like to do is laugh and share memes.

It might be a cute cat picture or other goofy jokes,

Or a ridiculous quote from some other funny folks!

Yo, I'm rapping about friends and you know it's happening,
Pack your sleeping bags and tents, y'all. It's time to go camping!
It's fun to hang with your **amigos** in the great outdoors,
Finding adventure, exploring, and making those s'mores.

About 40 million people camp in the United States each year.

Trying to find stuff to do? There's so much fun outside.

Get your friends, hop on a bicycle, and go for a ride.

Ride down some good trails, and get your legs pumping,

Some good exercise will always have your heart thumping!

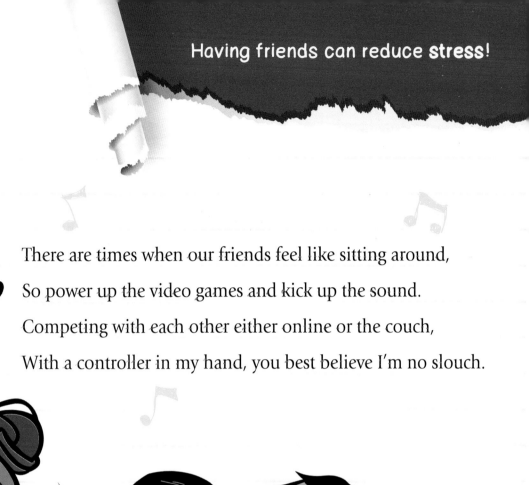

There are times when our friends feel like sitting around,

So power up the video games and kick up the sound.

Competing with each other either online or the couch,

With a controller in my hand, you best believe I'm no slouch.

Chapter 4
The Benefits of Friends

A friend is someone close who wants to hear your good news,

Who will be in your corner no matter which choice you choose.

A true friend will always be your biggest supporter,

And share your victories just like an evening news reporter.

There will be times in your life when things don't go so great,

When you're not feeling the best, like it was something you ate.

A great pal will still hang with you when times are tough,

They'll listen, give a hug, and all that other cheer-up stuff.

Some friends you've known since when you were a kid,

And they were around for some of the dumb things you did,

With you through and through, sharing the laughter and tears,

A true friend will be around for the rest of your years.

Some of your friends will come and then go,

They might move on or away—you just never know.

Treasure all your friendships, y'all, from the start to the end,

And be grateful for the person you call your best friend!

Chapter 5

Get in on the HiJinx

Rapping about friends is pretty easy. You and your friends could make up your own raps! First, write a list of the things you like doing together. Next, find words that rhyme with the stuff on your list. Try different words and speaking at different speeds. You'll be rapping about friends in no time!

Take It One Step More

1. Did you read the lines to a beat? If you didn't, tap your hand on your leg in a steady rhythm. Try reading the words in time to the beat. How does that change your understanding of the information?

2. Rapping is a form of musical poetry. Is rapping a good way to learn information?

3. Have someone else read the raps out loud. Do they put **accents** in the same places you do?

GLOSSARY

accent (AK-sent)—an emphasis put on part of a word

amigo (uh-MEE-go)—the Spanish word for friend

arithmetic (uh-RITH-muh-tik)—a science that deals with the addition, subtraction, multiplication, and division of numbers

galore (guh-LOR)—in large numbers or amounts

peer (PEER)—someone who belongs to the same societal group especially based on age, grade, or status

personality (per-suh-NA-lah-te)—the set of qualities that makes a person or animal different from others

peso (PAY-soh)—the money of Argentina, Chile, Colombia, Cuba, Dominican Republic, Mexico, Philippines, and Uruguay

stress (STRES)—something that causes strong feelings of worry or anxiety

yen (YEN)—the money of Japan

BOOKS

Bodden, Valerie. *Finding the Rhyme in a Poem.* Write Me a Poem. Mankato, MN: Creative Education, 2016.

Minden, Cecilia, and Kate Roth. *Writing a Poem.* Write It Right. Ann Arbor, MI: Cherry Lake Publishing, 2019.

Pearson, Yvonne. *12 Great Tips on Writing Poetry.* Great Tips on Writing. Mankato, MN: 12-Story Library, 2017.

WEBSITES

Friendship: Poems for Kids
poets.org/text/friendship-poems-kids

Holidays for Kids: Friendship Day
www.ducksters.com/holidays/friendship_day.php

Writing a Rap – Getting Started
www.youtube.com/watch?v=o6NZoTqWLq4

TIPS FOR WRITING YOUR RAPS

Rap about things you like. Make a list of activities you like to do or games you like to play.

To make your rap sound even better, practice it. Record yourself and listen to how it sounds. If it seems clunky, take out words your tongue trips over.

Never be afraid to change parts of your rap that don't work. Real rappers are always making edits to their rhymes. The more edits you do, the better your rap will be.